A Joke a Day Keeps the Doctor Away

BOB PHILLIPS

CARTOONS BY JONNY HAWKINS

HARVEST HOUSE PUBLISHERS

EUGENE, OREGON

Cover by Dugan Design Group, Bloomington, Minnesota

A JOKE A DAY KEEPS THE DOCTOR AWAY
Copyright © 2008 by Bob Phillips and Jonny Hawkins
Published by Harvest House Publishers
Eugene, Oregon 97402
www.harvesthousepublishers.com

ISBN-13: 978-0-7369-2257-9
ISBN-10: 0-7369-2257-1

Printed in the United States of America

08 09 10 11 12 13 14 15 16 / BP-NI / 10 9 8 7 6 5 4 3 2 1

Contents

1

Medical Mischief

Q: Why did the Eastern guru refuse novocaine when he went to the dentist?

A: *He wanted to transcend dental medication.*

Q: How many surgeons does it take to change a lightbulb?

A: *None. They'd wait for a suitable donor and do a filament transplant.*

Q: What is the difference between a magician and a psychiatrist?

A: *A psychiatrist pulls habits out of rats.*

Q: How can you tell if your doctor's a quack?

A: *By his large bill.*

Q: What's the difference between a surgeon and a puppy?

A: *If you put a puppy in a room by itself for an hour, it will probably stop whining.*

Q: Do psychologists have their own union?

A: *Of course they do. It's called the United Mind Workers.*

Q: Why do they put people into the insane asylum?

A: *For no reason at all.*

Q: How many doctors does it take to change a lightbulb?

A: *Depends on whether it has health insurance.*

Q: How many rational emotive behavior therapists does it take to change a lightbulb?

A: *Why should the lightbulb necessarily have to change? Why can't it be happy the way it is?*

The key to pedicatrics is in *treating* the patient.

Q: What do they call an intern who gets sick from reading medical textbooks?

A: *An ill-literate.*

Q: Why did the fisherman go to the doctor?

A: *He lost his herring.*

Q: Why did the bee go to the doctor?

A: *It had hives.*

Q: What illness is caused by the third letter in the alphabet?

A: *C-sickness.*

Q: Why did the banana go to the doctor?

A: *It wasn't peeling well.*

"Your wife just landed a big one, sir."

Q: What happened to the cowboy who began hearing voices in the middle of the cattle drive?

A: *He was deranged.*

Q: What do you call a surgeon with eight arms?

A: *A doctopus.*

Q: What kind of people enjoy bad health?

A: *Doctors.*

Q: What do you call a bone specialist from Egypt?

A: *A Cairopractor.*

Q: What is the coolest part of the human body?

A: *The hip.*

Q: What is the name of the famous doctor who is known for being lazy?

A: *Dr. Doolittle.*

"And if the motion sickness doesn't stop,
I recommend getting a car with bucket seats."

Q: What would you get if you crossed a massage therapist with a bully?

A: *Someone who really rubs you the wrong way.*

Q: What is a good name for an eye doctor?

A: *Iris.*

Q: Who performs the operations in a fish hospital?

A: *The head sturgeon.*

Q: How long should doctors practice medicine?

A: *Until they get it right.*

Q: What did Old MacDonald see on the eye chart?

A: *E-I-E-I-O.*

Q: What kind of teeth can you buy for a dollar?

A: *Buck teeth.*

"I made an appointment to get my iPod checked."

Q: What kind of specialist helps you stop sneezing?

A: *An achoo-puncturist.*

Q: Why did the house call for a doctor?

A: *Because it had window panes.*

Q: Where do you send a sick horse?

A: *To the horse-pital.*

Q: How can you tell if your neck is angry?

A: *You've got a sore throat.*

Q: What do you give a cowboy with a cold?

A: *Cough stirrup.*

Q: Why did the Christmas tree go to the hospital?

A: *It had tinsel-itis.*

"What do you mean I'm allergic to myself!?"

Q: How does a doctor make his money?
A: *By ill-gotten gains.*

Q: How do you know what a snake is allergic to?
A: *It depends on his medical hisss-tory.*

Q: Why did the tree go to the hospital?
A: *For a sap-pendectomy.*

Q: What do you call foot X-rays?
A: *Footographs.*

"Open your mouth and say, 'Arrrrrrgh.'"

2
Doctor, Doctor

Doctor, Doctor, I think I'm a smoke detector.
Don't worry. There's no cause for alarm.

Doctor, Doctor, I think I'm a parachute.
Come back tomorrow, I have no openings today.

Doctor, Doctor, I think I'm a goldfish. What should I do?
Here, take this tank-quilizer.

Doctor, Doctor, I think I'm a violin.
No wonder you're so high-strung.

Doctor, Doctor, I feel like a kangaroo.
Yes, you do seem a bit jumpy.

Doctor, Doctor, I think I'm a domino.
> *Oh, don't be such a pushover.*

Doctor, Doctor, I keep walking around and seeing double.
> *Keep one eye shut.*

Doctor, Doctor, I have a splitting headache.
> *I'll prescribe some aspirin and a pot of glue.*

Doctor, Doctor, can I have a second opinion?
> *Of course. Come back tomorrow.*

Doctor, Doctor, I'm boiling up.
> *Just simmer down.*

Doctor, Doctor, what did the X-ray of my head show?
> *Absolutely nothing.*

"I'll need a second opinion and I'd like to run your diagnosis past all the people in my chat room."

Doctor, Doctor, I keep thinking I'm a vampire.

Necks, please.

Doctor, Doctor, I think I'm an electric eel.

That's shocking.

Doctor, Doctor, I keep thinking I'm a caterpillar.

Don't worry. You'll soon change.

Doctor, Doctor, I think I'm a snake that is about to shed its skin.

Why don't you go behind the screen and slip into something more comfortable, then.

Doctor, Doctor, I think I'm an adder.

Great! You can help me with my accounts.

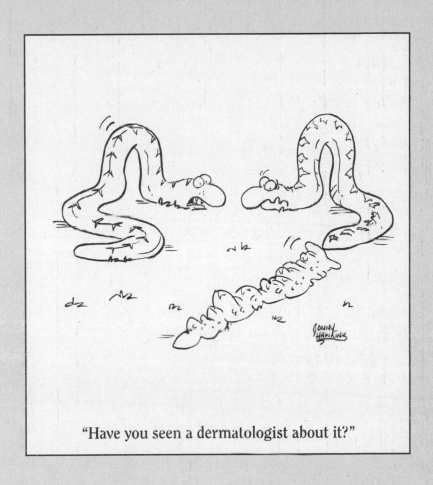

"Have you seen a dermatologist about it?"

Doctor, Doctor, I think I'm a yo-yo.

Are you stringing me along?

Doctor, Doctor, I've been fighting and fighting this cold, and it won't go away.

Never fight a cold. That only makes a cold sore.

Doctor, Doctor, my husband thinks he's a python.

I'll see if I can squeeze him in tomorrow.

Doctor, Doctor, I feel like a pair of socks.

Well, just don't get too dirty.

Doctor, Doctor, my stomach is sore.

Then teach it to be a good sport and call me in the morning.

"Ahh…you're a lumbar jack."

Doctor, Doctor, I'm having trouble breathing.

I'll put a stop to that.

Doctor, Doctor, everyone thinks I'm stupid.

That's ridiculous. Not everyone has met you yet.

Doctor, Doctor, I'm suffering from hallucinations.

I'm sure you are only imagining it.

Doctor, Doctor, I swallowed a roll of film.

Don't worry. Nothing will develop.

Doctor, Doctor, my sister thinks she's a squirrel.

Sounds like a nutcase to me.

Doctor, Doctor, I keep thinking I'm a fruitcake.

Stay away from Christmas parties.

"You have cabin fever."

Doctor, Doctor, what's good for biting fingernails?

Very sharp teeth.

Doctor, Doctor, I keep thinking I'm a joke.

Don't make me laugh.

Doctor, Doctor, how can I cure my sleepwalking?

Sprinkle tacks on your bedroom floor.

Doctor, Doctor, my tongue tingles when I use it to touch an unsalted peanut wrapped in used toaster oven aluminum foil. What's wrong with me?

You have far too much free time.

Doctor, Doctor, I think I'm a termite.

Get off that stool.

"He's a skilled carpenter, but he has this annoying habit of chewing his nails."

Doctor, Doctor, my husband smells like a fish.

Poor sole.

Doctor, Doctor, how long have I got?

Ten.

Ten what? Ten months? Ten weeks?

Ten, nine, eight, seven...

Doctor, Doctor, I think I'm a rubber band.

Why don't you stretch yourself out on the couch there and tell me all about it.

Doctor, Doctor, since the operation on my leg, I lean to the left.

I think you're all right.

Doctor, Doctor, sometimes I think there are two of me.

Good, you can pay both bills on the way out.

Doctor, Doctor, I always feel like a dog.

Sit down!

Doctor, Doctor, I'm nervous; this is the first brain operation I've had.

I know what you mean; it's the first I've performed.

Doctor, Doctor, I've got a little sty.

Then you'd better buy a little pig.

Doctor, Doctor, I think I'm Napoleon.

How long have you felt like this?

Ever since Waterloo.

Doctor, Doctor, my ear won't stop ringing.

Then answer it.

Doctor, Doctor, I keep thinking I'm a yo-yo.
I see. You're having ups and downs.

Doctor, Doctor, how do I stop my nose from running?
Stick out your foot and trip it up.

Doctor, Doctor, I feel like a sheep.
That's baaaaad!

Doctor, Doctor, I feel like a trash can.
Rubbish.

Doctor, Doctor, what is the best thing to take when you feel run down?
The license plate of the car that hit you.

"Postnasal drip runs in my family."

Doctor, Doctor, I tend to get fat in certain places. What should I do?

Stay away from those places.

Doctor, Doctor, I feel funny. What should I do?

Stop clowning around.

Doctor, Doctor, what's your best suggestion for this terrible bad breath I have?

Lockjaw.

Doctor, Doctor, will my chicken pox be better next week?

I don't make rash promises.

Doctor, Doctor, I can't sleep at night. What should I do?

Sleep during the day.

"He says he's feeling a little funny."

Doctor, Doctor, what should I do for water on the knee?

Wear pumps.

Doctor, Doctor, I'm worried about what kind of gifts Santa will bring me. Is there anything wrong with me?

Relax. Santa's sleigh just crashed, and we're treating him right now—he won't be out for a while.

Doctor, Doctor, do you think cranberries are healthy?

I've never heard one complain.

Doctor, Doctor, I think I'm a chimpanzee.

Stop monkeying around.

Doctor, Doctor, you have to help me. My wife thinks she's a pretzel.

Maybe I can straighten her out.

"You have water on the knee.
I'd continue with the flood pants."

Doctor, Doctor, my teenage son thinks he's a refrigerator.

Stay calm. I'm sure he'll chill out.

Doctor, Doctor, is the surgery going all right?

Oops—didn't mean to do that—er, I mean, yes, the surgery is going quite well.

Doctor, Doctor, I've got cuts and bruises all over my body. I was attacked by a huge beetle. It kicked, punched, and scratched me for about ten minutes.

Yes, there is a nasty bug going around.

Doctor, Doctor, I've got amnesia.

Just go home and forget all about it.

Doctor, Doctor, I feel like a twenty-dollar bill.

Go shopping. The change will do you good.

"We'll need you to sign this form that allows us to take heroic measures to find you some good food."

Doctor, Doctor, I can't stop stealing things.

Take these pills for a week, and if they don't work, get me a digital camera.

Doctor, Doctor, you've got to help me. Some mornings I wake up and think I'm Donald Duck. Other times I think I'm Mickey Mouse. Once in a while I even think I'm Pluto.

Hmmm, how long have you been having these Disney spells?

Doctor, Doctor, I keep thinking I'm a clock.

Don't get so wound up.

Doctor, Doctor, I keep thinking there are two of me.

One at a time, please.

Doctor, Doctor, I think I'm shrinking.

You'll have to be a little patient.

"Not bad for a first meeting."

Doctor, Doctor, I keep thinking I'm a spoon.

Just sit there and don't stir.

Doctor, Doctor, I can't stop singing "The Green Green Grass of Home."

That's what we doctors call the Tom Jones Syndrome.

Doctor, Doctor, I have hives all over me!

Now, now, no need to be rash.

Doctor, Doctor, I keep thinking I'm a bell.

Take these pills, and if they don't help, give me a ring.

Doctor, Doctor, I feel like a needle.

Hmmm, I see your point.

Doctor, Doctor, I keep thinking I'm a greyhound.

Take one of these pills every two laps.

Laura Ladle goes stir crazy.

Doctor, Doctor, I keep thinking I'm a bee.

Buzz off—can't you see I'm busy?

Doctor, Doctor, everyone thinks I'm a liar.

That can't be true.

Doctor, Doctor, I snore so loudly I keep myself awake.

Hmmm. Try sleeping in another room.

Doctor, Doctor, I think I'm a snail.

Don't worry. We'll soon have you coming out of your shell.

Doctor, Doctor, I just don't understand it! I feel like a deck of cards. What's wrong with me?

I don't have any idea. I'll deal with you later.

"Relax! Take some time off
and don't smell the flowers."

3
Bedside Manners?

People who think time heals everything haven't tried sitting it out in a doctor's waiting room.

A specialist is a doctor who has trained his patients to become ill during office hours.

Woman: Do I have Asiatic flu?

Doctor: No, you have Egyptian flu.

Woman: What is that?

Doctor: You're going to become a mummy.

The doctor felt the patient's purse and decided there was no hope.

Patient (calling very late at night): I can't sleep, Doctor. Can you do anything for me?

Doctor: Hold the phone for a minute, and I'll sing you a lullaby.

A minor operation is one performed on somebody else. A major operation is one performed on you.

His ailment is not chronic but a chronicle.

Stranger: Good morning, Doctor, I just dropped in to tell you how much I benefited from your treatment.

Doctor: But you're not one of my patients.

Stranger: I know. But my Uncle Bill was and I'm his heir.

Doctor: Why do you have V-37821 tattooed on your back?

Patient: That's not a tattoo. That's where my wife ran into me while I was opening the garage door.

"I do sutures. Are there any openings?"

Every chair in the doctor's waiting room was filled, and some patients were standing. At one point the conversation died down, leaving nothing but silence. During the silence, an old man stood up wearily and remarked, "Well, guess I'll go home and die a natural death."

Patient: I want the truth, Doctor. Am I going to get well?

Doctor: Why, of course you are. You're going to get well if it costs every cent you have.

Now they have megavitamins. Chew one bottle and you get enough strength to open the second bottle.

Doctor: Have your eyes ever been checked?

Patient: No, they've always been blue.

Patient: Am I getting better?

Doctor: I don't know. Let me feel your purse.

Patient: Doctor, people keep ignoring me.

Doctor: Next!

Patient: Doctor, I've only got 59 seconds to live.

Doctor: Wait a minute, please.

Patient: Doctor, my hair keeps falling out. What can you give me to keep it in?

Doctor: A shoebox. Next!

Patient: Doctor, doctor, I have a major hearing problem.

Doctor: How long have you had this problem?

Patient: No, I didn't go to my senior prom.

They just redecorated my friend's room. They put a new colored padding on the walls.

"You've been getting into my hair restorer, haven't you?"

Doctor: Well, your leg is swollen, but I wouldn't worry about it.

Patient: No, and if *your* leg were swollen, I wouldn't worry about it either.

One doctor said to the other, "Did you ever make a serious mistake in your diagnosis of a patient?"

"Yes," said the other doctor. "I once treated a patient for indigestion when he could have afforded an appendectomy."

A lady with a pain in her side went to see a doctor. He told her she had appendicitis and must have an operation. She decided to get another doctor's opinion. The second doctor told her she had heart trouble. "I'm going back to the first doctor," she replied. "I'd rather have appendicitis."

Consultation…a medical term meaning "share the wealth."

Patient: I didn't know that doctors still made house calls.

Doctor: Oh, I have another patient nearby. That way I kill two birds with one stone.

A patient limped into the doctor's office. The doctor handed the patient a large pill. Just then his nurse asked him a question. The patient limped over to the sink and choked down the pill. Then the doctor returned with a bucket and said, "Now drop the pill in the bucket and we'll soak your foot."

Patient: Doctor, what I need is something to stir me up. Something to put me in fighting trim. Did you put anything like that in this prescription?

Doctor: No. You will find that in the bill.

Joe: I'm afraid I can't afford that operation now.

Moe: It looks like you'll have to talk about your old one for another year.

The best way to cure your wife of nerves is to tell her it's caused by advancing age.

Doctor: Could you pay for an operation if I thought one was necessary?

Patient: Would you think one was necessary if I couldn't pay for it?

Doctor: I can do nothing for your sickness. It is hereditary.

Patient: Then send the bill to my father.

When the farmer was admitted into the doctor's office, he mumbled, "Shore hope I'm sick."

The doctor said, "That certainly is a poor attitude!"

"You see, Doc," replied the farmer, "I'd hate to feel like this if I'm well."

A toast for the Hay Fever Club... Here's looking at-choooooooooo.

Is it true that dermatologists make rash judgments?

+

Your doctor has prescribed a new medicine for your zjppzl condition. Take lrzgg a day before sdfghi and avoid pqaltn and rrtgww."

My husband was very sick, so we called Doctor Mowers. My husband took his medicine and got worse. Then we called Doctor Vernon, and my husband took his medicine but still got worse. We thought he was going to die, so we called Doctor Goodale, and he was too busy, and finally my husband got well.

Dr. Hanson: So the operation on the man was just in the nick of time?

Dr. Poure: Yes, in another 24 hours he would have recovered.

Doctor: I might be able to remove your mole in about a week.

Patient: Oh, thank you, Doc! That animal in my yard has been digging holes and driving me crazy.

Nurse: Doctor, there's a man in the waiting room who claims he's invisible.

Doctor: Tell him I can't see him.

"It's not a health risk, but I'd be
happy to remove your spot."

My doctor is an eye, ear, nose, throat, and wallet specialist.

Did you hear about the man who complained that every time he put on his hat he heard music? The doctor fixed him up. He removed the hat band.

My doctor is very unique. He grades me on my checkups and issues a bill in the form of a report card.

My doctor is a very generous man. He gave me four months to live. When I told him that I didn't think I would be able to pay his bill before I died, he gave me another six months.

Patient: Doc, am I going to die?

Doctor: Not as long as you have money in your bank
         account.

"There's a chance it might be hereditary."

Doctor: Say, the check you gave me for my doctor bill came back.

Patient: So did my arthritis!

Patient: Doctor, it's 2 AM and I can't sleep. It is the bill I owe you. I can't pay it. It bothers me so much that I can't sleep.

Doctor: Why did you have to tell me that? Now I can't sleep.

Patient: My right foot hurts.

Doctor: It's just old age.

Patient: But my left foot is just as old. How come it doesn't hurt?

Did you hear about the man who swallowed his glass eye and rushed to a stomach specialist? The specialist peered down the unfortunate fellow's throat and exclaimed, "I've looked into a lot of stomachs in my day, but I must say, this is the only one that ever looked back at me."

"Your check was a lemon, with a twist of lame."

Moe: This hearing aid I bought is the most expensive one on the market. It cost $2,500.

Joe: What kind is it?

Moe: Half-past four.

Addressing his students, the medical professor said, "Now notice how the muscle of the patient's leg has contracted until it is now much shorter than the other. Therefore, he limps. Now students, what would you do in such circumstances?"

One student replied, "I would limp too."

Sign in an obstetrician's office: *Pay as you grow.*

Have you noticed? First the doctor asks the patient what's wrong, and then the patient asks the doctor.

Since doctors have stopped making house calls, lots of patients now have to die without their help.

Nothing gives his friends more pleasure than when a health faddist becomes ill.

Healthy people have one thing in common: They always give advice to the sick.

A hypochondriac never recovers from any disease until he acquires another.

The only group of people who seem to have discovered the secret of long life are rich relatives.

Just once I'd like to say to that doctor, "You know, I'm not ready for you yet. Why don't you go back in that little office and I'll be with you in a moment. And get your pants off."
                                              —JERRY SEINFELD

It's not fun being a hypochondriac anymore. They have cured most of the good diseases.

Fortunately, my doctor doesn't believe in unnecessary surgery. Which means he won't operate unless he really needs the money.

Patient: Doctor, my irregular heartbeat is bothering me.

Doctor: Don't worry. We'll soon put a stop to it.

A new illness has been discovered. It is called "son-stroke." It is brought on by the reading of a will.

Doctor: So how are your broken ribs coming along?

Patient: Well, I keep getting this stitch in my side.

Doctor: Good, that shows the bones are knitting.

Have you heard about a new pill for hypochondriacs? It helps to increase the believability of imaginary illnesses. Unfortunately, it has some side effects. In fact, its primary function is to produce side effects.

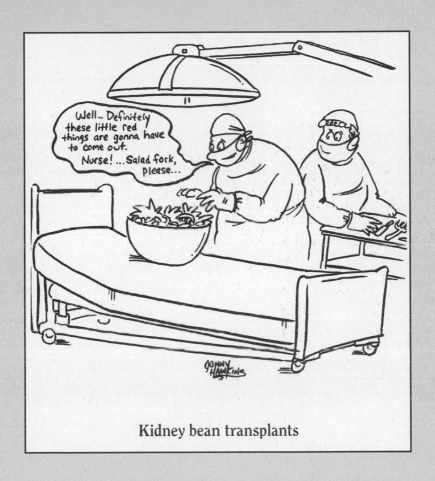

Kidney bean transplants

Why do doctors give pain pills? Shouldn't they be called relief pills?

Hay fever is much achoo about nothing.

Nobody is sicker than a man who is sick on his day off.

Before they admitted me to a private hospital, the doctor interviewed me to find out what illness I could afford to have.

They don't allow you to leave this private hospital until you're strong enough to face the accounts department.

It is a proven fact that you can learn a great deal about paranoids by just following them around.

I've got insomnia so bad, I can't even sleep when it's time to get up.

"I've been having some shooting pains, doc."

Did you hear about the man who accidentally swallowed all the tiles from a Scrabble set? His doctor told him that the problem would eventually sort itself out, but not in so many words.

Doctor: I have some good news and some bad news.

Patient: What is the good news?

Doctor: I'm going to buy a new BMW.

Patient: What is the bad news?

Doctor: You're going to help me pay for it.

Doctor: I have some good news and some bad news.

Patient: Give me the good news.

Doctor: They're going to name a new disease after you.

Patient: Doctor, those pills you gave me are great...but the only problem is, they make me walk like a crab.

Doctor: Yes, those are the side effects.

"Tobacco is unhealthy. I recommend you return to chewing your cud."

Did you hear about the podiatrist who ran for governor? He was defeated.

Joe: My family always followed the medical profession.

Moe: All doctors?

Joe: No, undertakers.

Patient: Doc, I've tried everything to stop smoking. I just can't do it.

Doctor: I'll prescribe one of those new nicotine patches.

Patient: It's no use. I've already tried that. I just couldn't keep the darn thing lit.

Don: I haven't been feeling too well, so I called my acupuncturist.

Griff: What did he say?

Don: He told me to take two safety pins and call him in the morning.

Friend: Is your husband still in the hospital?

Wife: Yes. He's in the Expensive Care Unit.

✚

Doctor: You'll have to stop drinking.

Patient: But Doc, I *need* water. What's next—are you going to ask me to stop *eating* too?

✚

Nurse: Open your mouth. This medicine doesn't taste bad.

Patient: Do you really expect me to swallow that?

✚

Patient: Why did you tell me to drink lemonade three times a day?

Doctor: It'll make you feel bitter.

✚

Patient: I ate clams for the first time in my life yesterday and now I'm sick.

Doctor: Maybe they were bad. How did the clams look when you opened the shells?

Patient: Opened them?

"Three hundred sixty-five cases of
wrinkle cream, please."

Patient: It's been two weeks since my last visit, and I still don't feel better.

Doctor: I don't understand it. Did you follow the instructions on the pills I gave you?

Patient: I sure did. It said, "Keep this bottle tightly closed."

Patient: I have a plan to make hair grow on bald men by feeding them natural cereal.

Doctor: Oh no! Not another hair bran scheme.

Doctor: How's that ringing in your ears—all gone since you took that medicine I prescribed?

Patient: Oh, yes, Doctor—now I just get a busy signal.

I went to the doctor and said, "Doc, every morning when I get up and look in the mirror, I feel like throwing up."

"What's wrong with that?" he said. "At least I know your eyesight is perfect."

It's not the minutes spent at the table that put on weight—it's the seconds.

A doctor is a general practitioner who calls in a specialist to share the blame.

Doctors are just the same as lawyers; the only difference is that lawyers merely rob you, whereas doctors rob you and kill you too.

Food isn't the only thing that causes indigestion: You can also get it from eating crow and swallowing your pride.

My insomnia is so bad that I couldn't even sleep during office hours.

Nurse: There is a man in the outer office with a wooden leg named Smith.

Doctor: What is the name of his other leg?

Patient: If a person's brain stops working, does he die?

Doctor: That's a silly question. You're alive, aren't you?

Doctor: Deep breathing helps destroy germs.

Patient: Okay. But how do I force them to breathe deeply?

Doctor: How long have you had this problem?

Patient: Two days.

Doctor: Why didn't you come see me sooner?

Patient: I did. That's how long I've been in your waiting room.

Reporter: Doctor, did you ever make a serious mistake?

Doctor: Yes. I once cured a millionaire in three visits.

I think it's only fair that a doctor who prescribes a placebo should be paid with counterfeit money.

"Thanks for your patience, Mr. Job."

Mary: Does your doctor make house calls?

Amy: Yes, but the house has to be very sick.

Patient: Doc, I need a prescription.

Doctor: For yourself?

Patient: No, it's for my fireplace.

Doctor: Your fireplace? What seems to be the trouble?

Patient: I think it has the flu.

Doctor: Strange—your brother is very small compared to you.

Patient: Of course. He's my half brother.

Bunny: Hey, Doc, how bad is it?

Doctor: Well, you've got a hare-line fracture.

"And you became a hairy potter?"

Doctor: You seem to be in excellent health, Mr. Hawkins. Your pulse is as steady and regular as clockwork.

Mr. Hawkins: That's because you've got your hand on my watch.

✚

Patient: Doctor, I have a burning stomach pain and a blazing fever.

Doctor: You don't need a doctor—you need a fireman.

✚

Patient: Hey, Doc, you've already removed my appendix, tonsils, and adenoids. Will I ever get out of this place?

Doctor: Don't worry, you're getting out...bit by bit.

✚

Patient: Doctor, I feel like 98 cents.

Doctor: That's ridiculous...you're as sound as a dollar.

Patient: Thanks for putting in your two cents' worth.

✚

"I assure you—these are standard exercises."

4
Those Crazy Psychiatrists

They say that one in every four Americans is unbalanced. Think of your three closest friends. If they seem okay, then you're in trouble.

The psychiatrist said sternly to the patient, "If you think you're walking out of here cured after only three sessions, you're crazy."

Psychiatrist: Congratulations, sir. You're cured.

Patient: Some cure. Before I was Julius Caesar. Now I'm nobody.

I used to be terribly conceited, but my psychiatrist straightened me out. Now I'm one of the nicest guys in town.

Patty: I asked my psychiatrist, "How soon until I know I'm cured?"

Patsy: What did he say?

Patty: He said, "The day you run out of money."

Patient: Doctor, I think I'm a pig.

Doctor: How do you feel otherwise?

Patient: Just sow-sow.

Patient: Doctor, my life is all messed up. I just don't think I can go on this way any longer.

Psychiatrist: Yes, yes, we all have problems. I can definitely help you, but it will take time. We'll start with four sessions a week. My fee is a hundred dollars an hour.

Patient: Well, that solves your problem. What about mine?

The psychiatrist said bluntly, "After listening to you for so many hours, I must tell you that you are really crazy."

The patient said, "I think I'd like a second opinion."

"All right. You're ugly too!"

John complained to his friend Joe that although he talked and talked, his psychiatrist never said a word.

A week later he told Joe he had a new problem: the analyst had died.

He replied, "What's the difference? Keep seeing him."

The latest thing in shock treatment is a psychiatrist who sends his bills in advance.

A modern murderer is supposed to be innocent until proven insane.

Patient: Doctor, Doctor, I think I'm Noah from the Bible.

Psychiatrist: You're the guy who says a flood's coming, right? Boy, you really *are* crazy.

Patient: Doctor, Doctor, I think I'm crazy.
Psychiatrist: So do I.

"Please! No more group hugs."

Patient: Doctor, Doctor, I think no one cares about me.

Psychiatrist: Did you say something?

Patient: Doctor, Doctor, I think I'm a walnut.

Psychiatrist: You do seem to be cracking up.

Patient: Doctor, Doctor, I feel like these sessions with you are one big joke.

Psychiatrist: Please don't say any more! I'm laughing so hard my sides are hurting!

Patient: Doctor, I think I'm Moses.

Doctor: Let your sickness go.

"How many paranoids does it take to change a lightbulb?"

"Why do you want to know?"

"Sometimes I don't feel you're fully committed to therapy."

Patient: Doctor, Doctor, I'm a schizophrenic.

Doctor: How long have you had this problem?

Patient: Please, I can't hear the doctor when you're all talking in my head!

You go to a psychiatrist when you're slightly cracked and keep going until you're completely broke.

—JOAN RIVERS

All analysts are psychological, but some are more psycho than logical.

A patient lies down on the couch, and the shrink says, "Okay, tell me what you dreamed last night."

"I didn't dream."

"How can I help you if you don't do your homework?"

Two analysts pass each other in the hall. One says, "Hello." The other thinks, "I wonder what he meant by that?"

"He ate his lunch money."

Brandy: I saw a psychiatrist today about my memory lapses.

Candy: Oh really? What did he say?

Brandy: He said I'd have to pay my bill in advance.

How many psychiatrists does it take to change a light-bulb?

One changes it—the other says, "Tell me what you *mean* by that."

The psychiatrist asked the exasperated mother: "Are you aware of any behavior problem your son may have?"

"I don't know…I've never seen him behaving," she replied.

The theme song of schizophrenia: "Do You Hear What I Hear?"

Here's the difference between the staff and the inmates at a psychiatric hospital: The staff have the keys!

"I wasn't aware of that."

How many psychologists does it take to change a lightbulb?

1. Just one, but the lightbulb really has to want to change.

2. None. The lightbulb will change itself when it's ready.

Patient: Doctor, I have a split personality.

Psychiatrist: Nurse, bring in another chair.

Patient: Doctor, I'm a manic depressive.

Psychiatrist: Why do you say that?

Patient: I calm down, cheer up, calm down, cheer up, calm down...

Patient: Doctor, people tell me I'm a wheelbarrow.

Psychiatrist: Don't let them push you around.

They now have a psychiatrist in Beverly Hills who specializes in inferiority complexes. He only takes patients with less than ten million.

Bill's wife had been right all along—
he had a screw loose.

Psychiatrist: Now, will you be able to pay this bill for the counseling I've given you?

Patient: Don't worry, Doc. You'll get the money or my name isn't King Henry VIII.

Is it true that they call the street where three psychiatrists live the mental block?

Now there's a list of the ten most neurotic people. It's called the best-stressed list.

I have been coming to your counseling sessions for two years and all you do is listen to what I have to say. You never say anything back. I didn't have to go to a psychiatrist for that. I could have stayed home with my husband. That's all he does too.

Psychiatrist: Well, you seem to have lost weight—did you take my advice?

Patient: Are you kidding? Carrots and celery are boring. I've been going to jog-through restaurants.

Two psychiatrists met in the street. One of them kept brushing his jacket.

"What's new?" asked one.

"Nothing, really, only I have these invisible insects crawling on me!"

"Well," said the other, jumping back, "don't brush them off on me!"

Late one night in the insane asylum one inmate shouted, "I am Napoleon."

Another said, "How do you know?"

The first inmate said, "God told me."

Just then, a voice from the next room shouted, "I did not."

Sign outside of psychiatrist's office: "Two Couches—No Waiting."

Sign outside of psychiatrist's office: "Guaranteed Satisfaction or Your Mania Back."

"We're an intervention group to stop others from intervening."

Wife: You have got to help me, Doctor. My husband keeps going around our house empting ashtrays. He even does it in public places. I can't stand it!

Psychiatrist: That's not at all unusual. Lots of people empty ashtrays.

Wife: Into their mouths?

✚

A psychologist is a man who, when a good-looking girl enters the room, looks at everybody else.

✚

A high school student wrote, "I would like to be a psychologist. I plan on taking as much psychology as possible in college and maybe someday emerge another Fraud."

✚

First Psychiatric Patient: I'm not feeling like myself today.

Second Psychiatric Patient: That makes four of us.

✚

Patient: Doc, I can't stop my compulsive buying.

Psychiatrist: Try emptying all the money in your bank account and make the check out to me.

Patient: Doc, I keep thinking I'm an airplane, and
            I'm afraid I'll try to fly off high buildings.

Psychiatrist: I'll delay the flight.

Psychiatrist: What times work best for you?

Obsessive Compulsive Patient:
            Monday, Tuesday, Wednesday, Thursday,
            Friday, Saturday, Sunday, Monday, Tuesday,
            Wednesday...

Insanity runs in my family. In fact, it practically gallops.

I'm confused. I have been having amnesia and déjà vu at the same time. In fact, I think that I have forgotten this before.

Insanity is doing the same thing over and over again and expecting different results.

"I'm afraid your reality check bounced."

I don't believe in temporary insanity as a murder defense. Temporary insanity is breaking into someone's home and washing and ironing all their clothes.

Did you hear the one about the ear of corn that went to a psychiatrist? It needed shuck treatment.

I think it's great to be depressed. You can behave as badly as you like.

A psychiatrist is a fellow who asks you a lot of expensive questions your wife asks for nothing.

Jack Sprat could eat no fat, his wife could eat no lean. A real sweet pair of neurotics.

—Jack Sharkey

Psychiatry enables us to correct our faults by confessing our parents' shortcomings.

"You live in a fantasy world by
constantly watching reality television."

Joe had been seeing a psychoanalyst for four years for treatment of his fear of monsters under his bed. It had been years since he had a good night's sleep. Furthermore, his progress had been very poor, and he knew it. So one day he stopped seeing the psychoanalyst and decided to try something different.

A few weeks later, Joe's former psychoanalyst met his old client in the supermarket and was surprised to find him looking well-rested, energetic, and cheerful. "Doc!" Joe said, "It's amazing! I'm cured!"

"That's great news!" the psychoanalyst replied. "You seem to be doing much better. How?"

"I went to see another doctor," Joe said enthusiastically, "and he cured me in just one session!"

"One?" The psychoanalyst couldn't believe it.

"Yeah," continued Joe, "my new doctor is a behaviorist."

"A behaviorist? How did he cure you in one session?"

"Oh, easy," Joe said. "He told me to cut the legs off my bed."

If someone ever catches you talking to yourself, the best thing to do is point at a chair and say, "He started it!" That way they won't think you're crazy.

A new patient confided to the psychiatrist, "I'd better tell you before we begin...I suffer from marked suicidal tendencies."

"Very interesting," nodded the psychiatrist, with his best professional nod of the head. "Under the circumstances then, I'm quite sure you wouldn't mind paying the bill in advance."

I gave up visiting my psychoanalyst because he was meddling too much in my private life.

A psychiatrist is a person who beats a psychopath to your door.

A man has a flat tire while driving down a desolate road in the middle of a dark and stormy night. After he gets out of the car, he curses in the rain and realizes he has stopped right next to a tall wire fence bearing a sign that reads Insane Asylum.

Though initially nervous, the man becomes really afraid when he notices that a light is on in one of the windows of the dark building and that someone is watching him. With shaking hands, he begins to jack up the car and remove the tire, all the while looking behind

his shoulder nervously. Then—in a flash of lightning—he sees a lone figure in pajamas and a bathrobe making his way toward him down the long path between the asylum and the fence. He begins to panic and tries to change the tire as fast as he can, hoping to get away before the figure reaches him, but his hands are shaking and the hex nuts are slick with rain.

Looking back over his shoulder, he sees the figure slowly coming closer. Finally, just as he removes the last nut, he looks over his shoulder and—in another flash of lightning—sees the horrible, distorted face of the lunatic, glaring at him from the other side of the fence, only a few feet away. Startled, the man yells, leaps back, and drops all of the metal nuts into a puddle of mud at his feet.

After a moment of tense, horrible silence, the lunatic says, "What's yer problem, mister?"

Stuttering with fright, the man burbles out, "Well, I...I got a flat tire and I...I lost all my hex nuts and now I can't even get the spare tire on."

The lunatic answers, "Why don't you just take one hex nut from the other three tires? That'll get you to the next town at least."

Surprised by the lunatic's apparent clarity, the man asks, "How'd you think of that?"

The lunatic answers, "Hey, I may be crazy, but I ain't stupid."

"Miss Melendy...the computer is down again... and this time it looks serious."

A doctor of psychology was doing his normal morning rounds when he entered a patient's room. He found the first patient sitting on the floor, pretending to saw a piece of wood in half. The second patient was hanging from the ceiling, by his feet.

The doctor asked the first patient what he was doing. The patient replied, "Can't you see I'm sawing this piece of wood in half?" The doctor asked the first patient what the second patient was doing. He replied, "Oh, he's my friend, but he's a little crazy. He thinks he's a lightbulb." The doctor looks up and notices the second patient's face is going all red.

The doctor tells the first patient, "If he's your friend, you should get him down from there before he hurts himself!"

The first patient replies, "What? And work in the dark?"

It's Time for You to Retire from Psychiatry When...

1. You diagnose your pets with various mental conditions, making notes like, "Fluffy is exhibiting signs of denial."
2. You begin to dream about treating imaginary patients, and when you're awake, you occasionally forget they're not real.
3. You start paying your own colleagues to have sessions with them.
4. You begin to wonder how you would treat easily angered fictional characters in a novel you're reading if you had them in an anger management setting.

5. A friend asks how you are doing, and you reply that you are experiencing "cognitive disarray" and cannot "adequately confront the tasks" before you today.
6. You are eating at a restaurant and begin to treat your waiter like one of your patients.
7. Your teenage daughter gets married, and you tell your friends you are "in denial" and "emotionally unbalanced" about letting her go.
8. Your patients start treating *you*.

Two Beverly Hills businessmen were discussing their doctors. The first said, "My psychiatrist is the strongest guy in the world. He could beat up your psychiatrist with one hand tied behind his back."

The second said, "Maybe, but my psychiatrist could cure yours of his aggressive behavior."

A man is walking along the street when he is brutally beaten and robbed. He lies unconscious, bleeding.

While he is lying there, a police officer passes by, but he crosses to the other side of the road without trying to help.

A boy scout troop does the same—as do many pedestrians.

Finally, a psychologist walks by and runs up to the man. He bends down and says, "Oh, no! Whoever did this needs help."

"That would explain the anxiety."

A big-game hunter recently returned from Africa and went to a psychiatrist. He told the psychiatrist he didn't want to go through analysis, but would pay him $200 if he would answer two questions.

The psychiatrist said this was highly irregular, but he agreed to do it.

"Is it possible," the hunter asked, "for a man to be in love with an elephant?"

"Absolutely impossible," the psychiatrist said. "In all the annals of medicine, I've never heard of it. The whole idea is ridiculous. What's your second question?"

Then the man asked meekly, "Do you know anyone who wants to buy a very large engagement ring?"

Patient: Doc, I have a morbid fear of thunder.

Psychiatrist: That's silly. You shouldn't be afraid of a thing like thunder. Why don't you just think of it as a drum roll from heaven?

Patient: Will that cure me?

Psychiatrist: Well, if it doesn't, do what I did: Stuff cotton in your ears, crawl under the bed, and sing "If You're Happy and You Know It."

"You are cold and distant."

A mother, visiting a department store, took her son to the toy department. Spying a gigantic rocking horse, he climbed up on it and rocked back and forth for almost an hour.

"Come on, son," the mother pleaded. "I have to get home to get your father's dinner."

The little lad refused to budge, and all her efforts were unavailing. The department manager also tried to coax the little fellow without meeting any success. Eventually, they called the store's psychiatrist out of desperation. He gently walked over and whispered a few words in the boy's ear, and the lad immediately jumped off and ran to his mother's side.

"How did you do it?" the mother asked incredulously. "What did you say to him?"

The psychiatrist hesitated for a moment, then said, "All I said was, 'If you don't jump off that rocking horse at once, son, I'll knock the stuffing out of you!'"

Wife: My husband thinks he's a refrigerator.

Psychiatrist: I wouldn't worry as long as he is not violent.

Wife: Oh, the delusion doesn't bother me. But when he sleeps with his mouth open, the little light keeps me awake.

"I worry about secondhand smoke from chimneys."

Judge: What possible excuse can you have for freeing this defendant?

Juror: Insanity.

Judge: All 12 of you?

The sad, quiet, big-eyed little lady sat in the psychiatrist's office. The good doctor questioned her gently as to why her family wanted her locked up.

"Now, tell me what your trouble is," he said.

"It's just that I'm so fond of pancakes, Doctor."

"Is that all? Why, I'm very fond of pancakes myself."

"Oh, Doctor, really? You must come over to our house. I've got trunks and trunks full of them."

One day, a patient walked into a psychiatrist's office and sat down. "Doctor," he said, "I've been having trouble sleeping. I keep thinking that tiny little men are going to grab me and take me away.

"Well," the psychiatrist said as he reached for the phone, "I think the men in the white coats are going to beat them to it."

One day, a well-to-do lady visited a mental hospital. As she was walking around, a distinguished-looking man offered his services as a guide on her tour.

In the course of several hours of careful inspection, the lady became impressed by the knowledge and intelligence of her guide. She was pleased by his gentle manners and obvious good breeding. In taking her leave, she thanked him and expressed her belief that the hospital was in good hands.

"Oh, but I am not a hospital official," the man said. "I'm a patient." He then told her how he had been unjustly committed by greedy members of his family who only had designs on his personal fortune. His detailed and reasonable account of the conspiracy touched the society woman's heart. She thought that it was a terrible wrong for the man to have been committed. She promised to get help and go to a judge to correct whatever injustice had been done. The kindly man thanked her for her warm kindness.

As she turned to go down the steps, she received a vigorous kick in the bottom. This caused her to stumble and nearly fall down the entire flight of stairs.

Gasping in shock, she turned toward the man and demanded, "Why did you do that? I might have been seriously hurt."

The patient smiled gently. "I didn't want to hurt you. I did that so you would not forget to tell the judge about my case."

"It wasn't all bad. They gave me an air splint
I can use in the bathtub."

Christmas Carols For Various Psychiatric Disorders

Borderline Personality Disorder:
  "Thoughts of Roasting on an Open Fire"

Dementia:
  "I Think I'll Be Home for Christmas"

Multiple Personality Disorder:
  "We Three Kings Disoriented Are"

Narcissistic:
  "Hark! The Herald Angels Sing About Me"

Paranoid:
  "Santa Claus Is Coming to Get Me"

Patient: Doctor, these crows are perched on the tops of fence posts around my garden every night. They just sit on top of the posts and watch me and watch me and watch me. What can I do?

Psychiatrist: That's easy—put a scarecrow in your yard to watch *them*.

Someone's lost their marbles.

A psychiatrist saw an old man pulling a box on a leash down a busy street. *Poor man*, he thought. *I'd better humor him.*

"That's a nice dog you've got there," he said to the old man.

"It isn't a dog. It's a box," said the man.

"Oh, I'm sorry," said the psychiatrist. "I thought you were a bit simpleminded at first," and he walked on.

The old man turned and looked at the box. "We sure fooled him, Rover," he said.

A man went into a gym to work out. While there, he sat next to a man lifting weights. "Say, buddy," he said. "Do you want to hear the latest joke about psychiatrists?"

The man gave him an angry look. "Look, buddy, I'm six foot three inches, I weigh 200 pounds, and I'm a psychiatrist. You see that guy over there? He's six foot six and weighs 250 pounds and can lift 300 pounds over his head. He is also a psychiatrist. The man on the treadmill is strong as an ox, and *he* is a psychologist. And the fellow doing leg presses with 400 pounds is a family counselor. Do you get the message?"

"I sure do," said the man. "I'll tell the joke slowly for you."

"Let's start with your pecs."

A patient said to his psychiatrist, "I'm dead."

"That's impossible," the psychiatrist replied. "You are talking to me right now."

"I'm dead."

The psychiatrist shook his head and decided to lead the patient out of his office and into a nearby bathroom with a full-length mirror. "Now," the psychiatrist began, "stand in front of that mirror and say these words over and over again for the next three hours: 'Dead men don't bleed.' Begin."

The patient did exactly as the psychiatrist told him, and when he was finished, the psychiatrist pricked the man's finger with a needle, causing it to bleed. "There now," said the psychiatrist. "What does that prove?"

Horrified, the patient looked up at the psychiatrist. "Dead men *do* bleed."

Ryan: This psychiatrist I've been seeing seems determined to convince me that I have some neuroses.

Jon: Why do you say that?

Ryan: If I'm early for an appointment, he says I have an anxiety complex. If I'm late, he says it is because I'm hostile. And if I arrive on time, he says that I'm being compulsive.

"I don't know, Doc…I'm just not a people person."

Psychiatric Hotline

Welcome to the Psychiatric Hotline.

- If you are *obsessive-compulsive,* please press 1 repeatedly.
- If you are a *codependent,* please ask someone to press 2 for you.
- If you have *panic disorder,* please keep pressing buttons until *something* works.
- If you have *multiple personalities,* please press 4, 5, and 7.
- If you are *bipolar,* please press 6 or 9, depending on your mood.
- If you are a *schizophrenic,* a small, quiet voice will tell you which number to press.
- If you are a *depressive,* it doesn't matter which number you press. No one will answer.
- If you have *paranoid delusions,* we know who you are and what you want. Just stay on the line so we can trace the call.

Thank you for calling the Psychiatric Hotline.

Irene: Who is that strange looking man who keeps staring at me?

Ivan: Oh, that's Dr. Don West, the famous expert on insanity.

"You exercised very heroic behavior by preventing the suicide of the patient in the bathtub," said the doctor. "I am confident that you are ready to be released from the asylum. The only thing I'm sorry about is that the patient later went on and hanged himself with a rope around his neck."

"Oh, no," said the patient. "He didn't kill himself. I had just hung him up to dry."

"I'm having an ethics implant."

5

The Dental Drill

I'm changing to a new dentist. I once asked the old one about my gum problem. He said, "Sorry. I don't have any on me."

Have you ever wondered about people who were so badly mutilated in an accident that they had to use dental records to identify them? How do they know who your dentist is?

You know you have bad breath when your dentist leaves the room and sends in a canary.

Did you hear about the dentist who went into the army? They made him a drill sergeant.

The first formal dance for dentists was called a gum ball.

When the first dentists' banquet was held, the meal cost $100 a plate…$50 for the upper and $50 for the lower.

Dave: That man wasn't a painless dentist like he adver-
 tised.

Jim: Why? Did he hurt you?

Dave: No, but he yelled when I bit his thumb, just like any other dentist.

One day a man went to see his dentist. During the examination, the man said, "My teeth are great. But let me tell you something. I never brush my teeth. I never use a rinse on my teeth: I never use a breath mint. I eat garlic all day long. And I've never had bad breath."

The dentist replied, "You need an operation."

"What kind of operation?"

"On your nose."

Dentist: What kind of filling would you like in your tooth?

Little Boy: Chocolate.

George was having trouble with a toothache, so he decided to visit the dentist.

"What do you charge for extracting a tooth?"

"Thirty-five dollars," replied the dentist.

"Thirty-five dollars for only two minutes' work?"

"Well," replied the dentist, "if you wish, I can extract it very slowly."

Dentist: Good grief! You've got the biggest cavity I've ever seen—the biggest cavity I've ever seen.

Patient: You don't have to repeat it, Doc!

Dentist: I didn't—that was the echo.

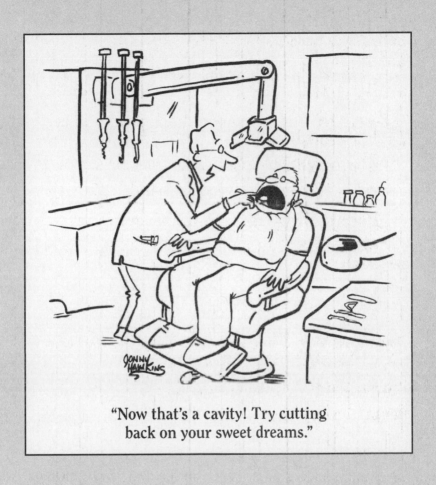

"Now that's a cavity! Try cutting
back on your sweet dreams."

6
A Diet a Day
Keeps the Fun Away

Diets are for people who are thick and tired of it!

A diet is a short period of starvation preceding a gain of five pounds.

The second day of a diet is a cinch. By the second day, you're off of it.

I've decided to stop worrying about what I eat. Why should I give up great food just to be able to spend three extra years in the geriatric ward.

A balanced diet is an ice cream cone in each hand.

Nothing arouses more false hopes than the first four hours of a diet.

I've been on a diet for three weeks. The only thing that I lost was three weeks.

Patient: I think I ate too much when I was at the beach party.

Doctor: Sounds like a bad case of eat-stroke.

Have you heard about the great new pasta diet? You walk past a bakery, past a candy store, past an ice-cream shop.

The hardest kind of diet pill to take is the thin person who tells you how to do it.

Diets are for people who have no taste buds.

"I did my personal best time running
to the donut shop."

I have a friend who just started the "A" diet. He can only eat food that begins with the letter "A": a steak, a chicken, a hamburger, a bowl of French fries...

When the first diet club was formed, it was a losing proposition.

The worst thing about a reducing diet is not watching *your* weight, but watching everyone else's.

Eat, drink, and be merry, for tomorrow we diet.

Doctors say that if you eat slowly, you eat less. You certainly will if you are a member of a large family.

He who does not mind his belly will hardly mind anything else.

When it comes to eating, help yourself more by helping yourself less.

We used to say "What's cooking?" when we came home from work. Now it's "What's thawing?"

If you really want to lose weight, there are only three things you must give up: breakfast, lunch, and dinner.

Did you ever notice that in bookstores you will find the diet books right between humor and fiction?

What's the use of going on a diet where you starve to death just to live longer?

Have you heard about the new garlic diet? You eat nothing but garlic. You don't lose weight, but people stand farther away, and you look thinner from a distance.

"I don't like the looks of this—my alphabet soup is
spelling out a Surgeon General's warning."

Ex-Dieter's Psalm

My stomach is my shepherd;

I shall not want low-calorie foods.

It maketh me to munch on potato chips and bean dip;

It leadeth me into 31 Flavors;

It restoreth my soul food.

It leadeth me in the paths of cream puffs in bakeries.

Yea, though I waddle through the valley of the shadow of dieting,

I will fear no skimmed milk;

For my appetite is with me;

My "Twinkies" and "Ding Dongs," they comfort me;

They anointeth my body with calories;

My scale tippeth over!

Surely chubbiness and contentment shall follow me

All the days of my life.

And I shall dwell in the house of Marie Callender Pies... forever.

Why does some of the food "health experts" allege is good for you taste like cardboard?

Dieting provides only temporary success on the scale and misery to the dieter.

You Know It Is Time for a Diet When...

- You dive into a swimming pool so your friends can go surfing.
- You have to apply your makeup with a paint roller.
- Your weight loss group demands your resignation.
- You step on a penny weight scale that gives you your fortune, and it says, "One at a time, please!"
- Your face is so full that you look like you're wearing horn-rimmed contact lenses.
- The bus driver asks you to sit on the other side because he wants to make a turn without flipping over.
- You're at school in the classroom and turn around and erase the entire blackboard.
- They throw marshmallows at your wedding.
- You get a hiccup in your bathing suit, and it looks like someone adjusting a Venetian blind.
- You fall down, try to get up, and rock yourself to sleep in the process.
- A shipbuilder wants to use you as a model.
- You step on a penny weight scale that gives you your fortune, and it says, "You are very fond of food. You lack willpower, and you overdo everything. Either that, or a baby elephant has just collapsed on this scale."

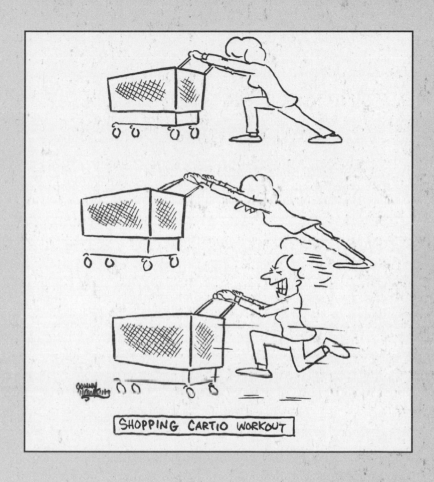

SHOPPING CARTIO WORKOUT

They all say the best way to lose weight is to eat all you want of everything you don't like.

A diet helps a person gain weight more slowly.

To diet, or not to diet—that is the question.

Whether 'tis nobler in the mind to suffer the slings and arrows

Of soda and potato chips;

Or to take arms against a sea of calories,

And by opposing, lose them? To diet, to fast;

No more; and by a fast to say we end

The plumpness and the thousand natural pounds

That flesh is heir to. 'Tis a consummation

Devoutly to be wish'd. To diet or fast;

To fast: perchance to lose—ay, there's the rub;

For in that one diet what loss may come

When we have shuffled off this excess weight,

Must make us thin.

A husband was standing on the bathroom scales, desperately holding his stomach in.

His wife, thinking he was trying to reduce his weight, remarked: "I don't think that will help."

Her husband replied, "It's the only way I can read the numbers on the scale."

An older couple both died in an auto accident and were being shown around heaven by St. Peter. They couldn't believe how fabulous heaven was. There were swimming pools, permanent sunshine, tennis courts, and all the ice cream you could eat.

"Well, Marge," hissed the husband, "we could have been here ten years ago if you didn't feed me all those fancy low-fat diets."

7

Long and Healthy

Caffeine Is My Shepherd

Caffeine is my shepherd; I shall not doze.

It maketh me to wake up in lecture halls,

It leadeth me beyond the sleeping masses.

It restoreth my buzz.

It leadeth me in the paths of consciousness

For its name's sake.

Yea, though I walk through the valley of the shadow of addiction,

I will fear no decaf.

For my coffee cup is with me.

My cream and sugar, they comfort me.

They preparest a tall latte before me in the presence of fatigue.

Caffeine anointeth my day with pep; my mug runneth over.

Surely richness and taste shall follow me all the days of my life,

And I will dwell in the house of Starbucks forever.

A pretty young girl had broken off her engagement with a young doctor.

"Do you mean to tell me," exclaimed her girlfriend, "that he actually asked you to return all his presents?"

"Not only that," she replied. "He sent me a bill for 35 house calls."

Doctor: Ever had a serious illness?

Patient: No.

Doctor: Ever had an accident?

Patient: No.

Doctor: You mean you have never had a single accident in your life?

Patient: Never.

Doctor: Wow! You mean you've never once been seriously hurt?

Patient: Well, actually, last spring a bull tossed me over a fence.

Doctor: Well, don't you call that an accident?

Patient: No, sir! He did it on purpose.

An elderly gentleman wasn't feeling well, and he became irritated with his doctor because he wasn't getting better after five visits.

"Look! I'm doing all I can to help you," said the doctor. "I can't make you younger."

"I wasn't particularly interested in getting younger," said the old man. "I just want to continue growing older."

George the truck driver was starting to feel sleepier and sleepier as he made his trips, so he decided to go see his doctor about it. When he entered his doctor's office the next day, he explained his problem. "Is there anything you can do to help me?"

"Sure," said the doctor. "Try this energy drink and come back next week."

George took the drink and left.

Next week, George came back with dark circles under his eyes.

"My goodness," the doctor said. "Did you try the energy drink?"

"That drink sure has a lot of energy, Doc. Once I walked out the door last week, it hopped out of my hand and ran out the building."

Doctor: Please look these shoes over and see if they are worth repairing.

Cobbler: No, they are not.

Doctor: Thank you.

Cobbler: That will be three dollars.

Doctor: For what? You haven't done anything.

Cobbler: Neither did you the other day when you examined me and charged me 35 dollars after telling me you found nothing wrong with me.

A bunch of workers were busy building a home for a rich doctor they all knew. Instead of helping the workers, however, the doctor was content to sip his glass of lemonade at a picnic table and enjoy the relaxing sunshine. Since the workers were not doing this for money and were helping the doctor build his home as a favor to him, many became rather disgruntled. One construction worker said to the other, "Hey, how come he gets lemonade, and we don't? Who made him the privileged boss all of a sudden?"

"I don't know," the other one said. "Why don't you go over to him and find out?"

So with determination, the construction worker marched right up to the doctor and asked, "Why aren't you helping us or sharing your lemonade? You aren't paying us for this job, after all."

The doctor yawned lazily and set his lemonade gently

When grammarians become doctors

down on the table. "Well, it has a little something to do with intelligence."

The worker scratched his head. "Intelligence? What's that?"

"Follow me. I'll show you."

The doctor led the confused worker to a tall, wide oak tree. Then the doctor placed his hand in front of the tree and said to the worker, "Here, hit my hand with your shovel."

"Huh?"

"You heard me. Hit my hand with your shovel."

"Well, all right."

With that, the construction worker swung his shovel as hard as he could toward the doctor's hand. Just in time, the doctor withdrew his hand, causing the worker to hit the tree so hard with his shovel that he shook for a full minute. Laughing, the doctor said, "See? That's what I mean by 'intelligence.' I didn't get my medical degree with my muscles, you know."

Jarred but enlightened, the construction worker went back to the house where the other workers were. One worker leaned on his shovel and asked him, "Well? What did you find out?"

"I learned something about intelligence."

"Intelligence? What's that?"

"Here," the construction worker said, placing his hand in front of his face. "Hit my hand with your shovel."

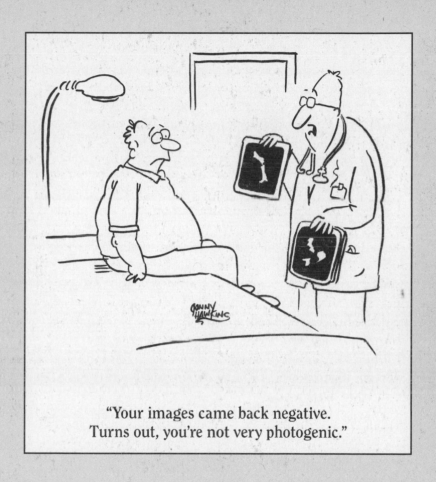

"Your images came back negative.
Turns out, you're not very photogenic."

Socialized Medicine

Here is a sample of what might happen if we had socialized medicine currently making the rounds:

A man feeling the need of medical care went to the medical building. Upon entering the front door, he found himself faced with several doors, each marked with the names of ailments such as appendicitis, heart disease, cancer, and so on.

He felt sure his trouble could be diagnosed as appendicitis, so he entered the door so marked. Upon entering, he found himself faced with two more doors, one marked male and the other female. He entered the door marked male and found himself facing two more doors, marked taxpayer and non-taxpayer. He still owned equity in his home, so he went through the door marked taxpayer, and found himself confronted with two more doors marked single and married.

He had a wife at home, so he entered the proper door and once more there were two more doors, one marked Republican and the other Democrat.

Since he was a Republican, he entered the door and promptly fell nine floors to the alley.

A man sought medical aid because he had popped eyes and a ringing in the ears. A doctor looked him over and suggested removal of his tonsils. The operation resulted in no improvement, so the patient consulted another

"Stop calling it parts and labor!"

doctor who suggested removal of his teeth. The teeth were extracted but still the man's eyes popped and the ringing in his ears continued.

A third doctor told him bluntly, "You've got six months to live." In that event, the doomed man decided he'd treat himself right while he could. He bought a flashy car, hired a chauffeur, had the best tailor in town make him 30 suits, and decided even his shirts would be made-to-order.

"Okay," said the shirt maker, "let's get your measurement. Hmm, 34 sleeve, 16 collar."

"Fifteen," the man said.

"Sixteen collar," the shirt maker repeated, measuring again.

"But I've always worn a 15 collar," said the man.

"Listen," the shirt maker said, "I'm warning you. You keep on wearing a 15 collar and your eyes will pop and you'll have a ringing in your ears."

Patient: What are your fees, doctor?

Doctor: I charge 35 dollars for the first visit and 25 for the second visit.

Patient: Well, doctor, it's nice to see you again! What should I do?

Doctor: Take the same medicine I gave you last time.

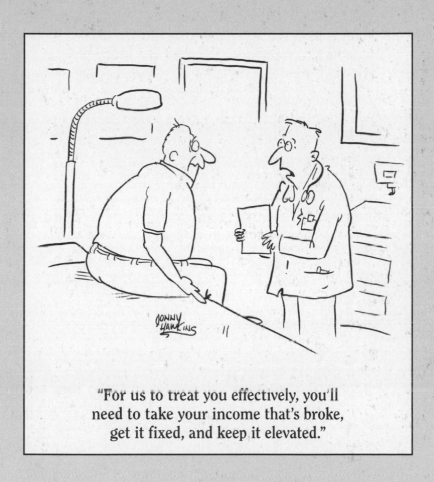

A doctor was called in to see a very busy patient.

"Well, sir, what's the matter?" he asked cheerfully.

"That's for you to find out," the patient snapped.

"I see," said the doctor. "Well, if you'll excuse me a minute, I'll phone a friend of mine...a veterinarian. He's the only man I know who can make a diagnosis without asking a single question."

One doctor had a patient with blindness in both eyes. When the patient wheeled into the hospital in a wheelchair one day, a receptionist asked him, "Is there anything I can do for you? Where do you need to go?"

"ICU," the patient said.

The receptionist called for a nurse.

The nurse asked the man, "Where do you need to go, sir?"

Again, the patient said, "ICU."

She quickly wheeled him into his doctor's office, and she told the doctor that the patient felt he needed to go to the intensive care unit. The doctor nodded and scribbled some notes furiously.

"ICU," the patient repeated.

"Yes, yes, I know," said the doctor. "We'll get you to the ICU shortly."

"No," said the patient, exasperated. "I'm trying to tell you I'm not blind anymore. I *see* you!"

A medical student was asked how much of a certain drug should be administered to a patient. The young man replied, "Five grains."

A minute later he raised his hand. "Professor," he said, "I would like to change my answer to that question."

The professor looked at his watch and replied, "Never mind. Your patient has been dead for forty seconds."

Doctor: Well, I'm told that you have a severe memory problem.

Patient: Yes, that's correct.

Doctor: All right, then. How long have you had this problem?

Patient: I can't remember.

Doctor: I see.

Patient: What do you see?

Doctor: Uh, I see that you can't remember.

Patient: Can't remember what?

Doctor: You can't remember how long you've had this problem.

Patient: What problem?

Doctor: Your memory problem.

Patient: When did I get a memory problem?

"I see the ring in your ear has moved to your nose."

Doctor: (Trying not to get exasperated) You just *told* me you have a memory problem.

Patient: I did?

Doctor: Yes, you did.

Patient: Oh.

Doctor: Anyway, what sorts of things *can* you remember?

Patient: Well, I can't remember.

Doctor: Wait, what? You can't remember which things you *can* remember?

Patient: If I could remember what I *can't* remember, I'd be able to tell you what I can't remember, now couldn't I?

Doctor: Can you remember anything?

Patient: Hmm… I can't remember if I remember anything or not.

Doctor: Then I suppose you *can't* remember anything.

Patient: I didn't say *that*.

Doctor: But you implied it.

Patient: Implied what?

Doctor: (Putting his head in his hands in frustration) I can't remember.

"Honey, have you seen that book I was just looking at?"

You Thought You Had a Bad Day?

Dear Sir:

When I got to my son's dorm room, I found that his attempted remodeling had left DVD player parts all over the place. Don't ask. So I went to the store to pick up extra DVD player parts and began to reassemble the DVD player. When I had fixed the DVD player, I had a lot of parts left over, so I went to the bottom of the dorm complex, and I threw them in the dumpster. Unfortunately, a dump truck was picking up the dumpster as I leaned forward into it unaware of what was happening, so I ended up being lifted off the ground with the dumpster and tossed into the truck.

When the truck reached its destination, it dumped me over a bunch of broken glass, leaving me with deep cuts all over. I proceeded to slip on the glass and tumble down a heap of trash, dislocating my shoulder—my elbow then accidentally pushed a button on a remote which activated a nearby forklift carrying a load of bricks, spilling them all over me.

As I crawled out of the pile of bricks, another dump truck dropped *another* load on me, causing my back to give out.

When I finally made my way out of the pile and tried to stand up as best as I could, I slipped on a banana peel, landed on the remote, activated the forklift again, and was knocked out as it rammed into me, putting me in the hospital.

I respectfully request sick leave.

Signed,

Ouch

"The crash-test results are back...
you're making an impact."

"Doctor," said the pale-faced man to his physician. "I'm in an awful state! Whenever the phone rings, I almost jump out of my skin. The doorbell gives me the willies. If I see a stranger at the door, I start shaking. I'm even afraid to look at a newspaper. What's come over me, anyway?"

The doctor patted him on the back sympathetically. "There, there, old man. I know what you're going through. My teenaged daughter just learned to drive too."

My husband, a marriage counselor, often refuses to accompany me to parties and get-togethers. He says that so many people spoil his evening by asking him for advice. One day I saw my doctor, and I asked him if this happened to him also. He told me that it happened to him all the time. I then asked him how he got rid of those people.

"I have a wonderful remedy," the doctor grinned. "When someone begins to tell me his ailments, I stop him with one word: 'Undress.'"

A man who was in the hospital for a week noticed that several pretty nurses were wearing a pin that looked like a small apple.

Being curious he asked, "What does that apple pin signify?"

"Nothing special," said one of the nurses. "We just wear it to keep the doctors away."

"Your heart rate, blood pressure, and insurance deductible are all alarmingly high."

Patient: Doctor, I've got trouble with my throat.

Doctor: Go in the other room and disrobe. I'll be there in a minute.

Patient: But, doctor, it's just my throat!

Doctor: Get in the other room and disrobe, and I'll examine you.

So the man went in and disrobed. As he was sitting there in his shorts, he looked around. Next to him was another guy sitting there in his shorts also, with a big package in his hands.

The patient said, "Can you imagine that doctor? I've got trouble with my throat, and he tells me to disrobe!"

The other man replied, "What are you complaining about? I came in here only to deliver a package."

The Joys of Staying Fit

- You're always "on the run."
- You get to feel sore every day and lie about how great it feels.
- Marathons are always suspenseful.
- You never have to worry about eating those unpleasant *sugary* foods again.

"I find that hard to swallow."

A draftee went in for his physical wearing a truss and with papers that were stamped "M.E." for Medically Exempt.

Afterward a friend borrowed the truss to wear for his physical.

At the end of the examination the doctor stamped M.E. on his papers.

"Does that mean I'm 'medically exempt'?" he asked the doctor.

"No," replied the doctor. "M.E. stands for Middle East. Anyone who can wear a truss upside down can ride a camel."

A patient tells his doctor his arm talks to him.

"Don't be ridiculous," the doctor says.

"No, really, it does," protests the patient. "Just listen to it."

The doctor puts his stethoscope to the man's arm and is amazed to hear the arm say, "Hey, can you lend me twenty dollars?"

The doctor says, "It's okay. It's just broke."

"My hairdresser and my manicurist have dissenting opinions of your diagnosis. If you wouldn't mind, I'd like to speak to your barber."

Doctor: (The doctor called Griff to let him know the results of his physical exam.) Griff, I've got bad news and worse news. The bad news is that you have 24 hours to live.

Griff: Oh no! That's bad, but what could possibly be worse than that?

Doctor: I've been trying to get you since yesterday!

Patient: Doctor, I don't know what's wrong with me. Everything hurts. If I touch my shoulder just here, it hurts. If I touch my leg just here, it hurts. If I touch my leg here, it hurts. And if I touch my head here, it hurts.

Doctor: It sounds like you've got a broken finger.

The doctor didn't stay long with the patient. As he left the house, he told the patient's wife, "There's nothing wrong with your husband. He just thinks he's sick."

A few days later the doctor called to check to see if his diagnosis had been correct. He asked the wife, "How's your husband today?"

"He's worse," said the wife. "Now he thinks he's dead."

"Amazing. I just downloaded love
songs onto my stethoscope."

A doctor was called into court as an expert witness in a murder case.

Lawyer: Doctor, before you performed the autopsy, did you check for a pulse?

Doctor: No.

Lawyer: Did you check for breathing or blood pressure?

Doctor: No.

Lawyer: So, then it's possible that the victim was alive when you began the autopsy?

Doctor: No. His brain was sitting on my desk in a jar at the time.

Lawyer: But could the patient have been alive nevertheless?

Doctor: Well, I suppose it's possible. He may still be out there practicing law somewhere.

A Little Known Fact

- There are 700,000 doctors in the United States.
- Doctors cause 120,000 accidental deaths each year.
- That works out to 0.171 deaths per physician (U.S. Department of Health & Human Services).
- There are 80,000,000 gun owners in the United States.
- There are 1,500 accidental gun deaths per year.
- That works out to 0.0000188 accidental deaths per gun owner.
- Statistically doctors are approximately 9,000 times more dangerous than gun owners.

Doctor: I'm afraid you only have six months to live.

Patient: Six months? But I'm only 42 years old!

Doctor: I'm very sorry. I suggest you make the most of the time you have left.

Patient: I think I'll go live with my mother-in-law for the next six months.

Doctor: I don't understand. That sounds very unusual. Are you sure you want to do that?

Patient: Yep. It will be the longest six months of my life.

One day a man said to his doctor, "Doctor, can you please help me out? I think my wife is going deaf and I'm not sure what to do about it."

The doctor replied, "Well, the first thing to do is to see how bad your wife's hearing really is. Stand a distance from her and ask her a question. If she doesn't respond, move a little closer and ask the question again. Keep repeating this procedure until she finally answers you. Then you will have some idea how bad her hearing is."

The man went home and followed the doctor's advice. From the other room he said, "Honey, what's for dinner?"

She didn't respond so he moved a little closer.

He asked the question again. "Honey, what's for dinner?"

Still there was no answer. He kept on doing this over

"Did you fill out your organ donor card?"

and over and moving closer and closer to her. Eventually, he was standing two feet behind her, and he asked the question again. His wife finally turned around, put her hands on her hips, and said, "For the ninth time, I said we're having fried chicken!"

Leaders at a local hospital wanted to build a new wing to add more care for their patients. The leaders thought that they would go to the doctors who worked at the hospital and ask them for contributions. The following was the response they received.

- The *allergists* voted to scratch it.
- The *cardiologists* didn't have the heart to say no.
- The *dermatologists* preferred no rash moves.
- The *gastroenterologists* had a gut feeling about it.
- The *internists* thought it was a hard pill to swallow.
- The *neurologists* thought the administration had a nerve.
- The *obstetricians* stated they were laboring under a misconception.
- The *ophthalmologists* considered the idea short-sighted.
- The *orthopedists* issued a joint resolution.
- The *pathologists* yelled, "Over my dead body!"
- The *pediatricians* said, "Grow up!"
- The *plastic surgeons* said, "This puts a whole new face on the matter."
- The *podiatrists* thought it was a big step forward.
- The *proctologists* said, "We are in arrears."

"Don't get caught in the headlights or you may suffer from the exposure to SUV rays."

- The *psychiatrists* thought it was madness.
- The *radiologists* could see right through it.
- The *surgeons* decided to wash their hands of the whole thing.
- The *urologists* felt the scheme wouldn't hold water.

A woman went with her husband to the doctor to see what was wrong with him. After the checkup, the doctor pulled the wife aside into a separate office and said, "I'm afraid that I have some bad news. Your husband is a very sick man. The only way he is going to get well is if you cook three hearty meals for him every day for a year. Also, you need to give him a back rub twice a day. He must not be burdened with any household chores or yard maintenance. He shouldn't even put out the effort to pay monthly bills. The house must be kept spotless with absolutely no dust at any time. He cannot help you with the children, and there must not be any yelling, slamming of doors, or loud music. He shouldn't even answer the telephone. And it would be very beneficial if you would say kind words to him many times during the day and ask him if there is anything you can get for him. Do you have any questions?"

"Just one." said the wife. "You mean I have to do all of this for one year?"

"Yes, that is correct," replied the doctor.

The lady then left the doctor and joined her husband and didn't say anything. On their way home from the doc-

"I'm afraid they're not goose bumps—
it's chicken pox."

tor's office the husband asked, "What did the doctor say to you when he talked with you alone in the other office?"

"He said, 'I'm afraid I have some bad news.'"

"What did he say?" asked the husband.

"He said you're going to die."

Other Books by Bob Phillips

All-Time Awesome Collection
of Good Clean Jokes for Kids

The Awesome Book
of Bible Trivia

The Awesome Book
of Heavenly Humor

Awesome Good Clean
Jokes for Kids

Awesome Knock-Knock
Jokes for Kids

The Best of the Good
Clean Jokes

Dude, Got Another Joke?

Extremely Good Clean
Jokes for Kids

Fabulous and Funny
Clean Jokes for Kids

Good Clean Jokes to Drive
Your Parents Crazy

Good Clean Knock-Knock
Jokes for Kids

How Can I Be Sure?

How to Deal with
Annoying People

Jolly Jokes for Older Folks

Laughter from
the Pearly Gates

Over the Hill & On a Roll

Over the Next Hill
& Still Rolling

Over the Top Clean
Jokes for Kids

Overcoming Anxiety
and Depression

Super Incredible Knock-
Knock Jokes for Kids

The World's Greatest
Collection of Clean Jokes

The World's Greatest
Knock-Knock Jokes for Kids

For more information, send a self-addressed
stamped envelope to:

Family Services
P.O. Box 9363
Fresno, California 93702

Books by Jonny Hawkins

HARVEST HOUSE BOOKS BY JONNY HAWKINS

The Awesome Book of Heavenly Humor

A Joke a Day Keeps the Doctor Away

Laughter from the Pearly Gates

OTHER PRODUCTS FROM JONNY HAWKINS

Cheap Laughs for Church Publications

CALENDARS

Medical Cartoon-a-Day Calendar

Fishing Cartoon-a-Day Calendar

Cartoons for Teachers

Laughter Shocks

The Ultimate Chuckle-a-Day Edition

For more information, contact:

jonnyhawkins2nz@yahoo.com